EVERYONE'S JOB
REPAIRING DAMAGED RELATIONSHIPS

EVERYONE'S JOB
REPAIRING DAMAGED RELATIONSHIPS

N. DANE TYNER

XULON PRESS

Xulon Press
2301 Lucien Way #415
Maitland, FL 32751
407.339.4217
www.xulonpress.com

© 2020 by N. Dane Tyner

All rights reserved solely by the author. The author guarantees all contents are original and do not infringe upon the legal rights of any other person or work. No part of this book may be reproduced in any form without the permission of the author. The views expressed in this book are not necessarily those of the publisher.

Unless otherwise indicated, Scripture quotations taken from the Holy Bible, New International Version (NIV). Copyright © 1973, 1978, 1984, 2011 by Biblica, Inc.™. Used by permission. All rights reserved.

Scripture quotations taken from the New King James Version (NKJV). Copyright © 1982 by Thomas Nelson, Inc. Used by permission. All rights reserved.

Paperback ISBN-13: 978-1-6628-0647-6

Ebook ISBN-13: 978-1-6628-0648-3

CONTENTS

Introduction vii
Chapter 1: Relationships Can Be Challenging 1
Chapter 2: Six Crucial Components of Reconciliation 7
    1. Confrontation
    2. Confession
    3. Forgiveness
    4. Restitution
    5. Rebuilding Damaged Trust
    6. Acceptance

Chapter 3: Three Problems Related to the
Reconciliation Process 31
    1. Sinful Confrontations
    2. Faulty Confessions
    3. Faulty Forgiveness

Chapter 4: Closing Thoughts 39
Addendum: Be Reconciled to God 45
How to be sure you are in right relationship with the Maker

The Author's Invitation 53
Zoom opportunity with the author

About the Author 55

Acknowledgments 57

INTRODUCTION

You may be unemployed or retired, yet nevertheless you have an important job. You may be holding down one, two, or even three jobs to make ends meet; but you, too, have yet another job. That job is repairing damaged relationships.

We live in a world of damaged relationships. Not all relationships are antagonistic, of course, but we all live with the realization that badly strained and even badly broken relationships are all too common. In addition to those obviously strained or alienated relationships, many other relationships are devoid of significant depth (where depth should be expected); invisible forces seem to keep these relationships safe by keeping them superficial. Indeed, relationships in need of restoration are easily found by all who would see.

As a Christian minister for over forty years, I have served mostly in the role of a family counselor. Throughout these years, I have encountered hundreds of people who are greatly confused about their damaged relationships. They usually know their relationships are messed up but often don't know what to do about it. Their confusion often leads them to a helper like me. Surprisingly, other people are clueless about how messed up some of their relationships really are. Often, however, these people are in relationships with someone who is not so blind.

If you have damaged relationships, you are not alone. If you're confused, you are not alone. I write to bring you hope and clarity. The confidential sanctuary of the counseling office has enabled me to get to know—deeply know—many people and thereby to clearly see the manifold struggles with relationships we all can have. These experiences, as well as formal education experiences, have equipped me to address this vital subject.

I expect that my writing will help you find clarity—clarity that will enable you to both *understand* and *act* on truth. I have experienced freedom in my own life through understanding and acting on the very truths I share here. Because of this, I hope to enable others to find the freedom Jesus made available to all of us. The availability of full freedom is the *full gospel*. Jesus doesn't offer us something only for the sweet by-and-by; He wants to help us overcome in the nasty here-and-now!

Just as we are aware of damaged relationships in our lives, we are also likely aware of relationships that once were hostile but are no longer so. A restored relationship has been achieved. The biblical word commonly used for this process of restoration is *reconciliation*. The two parties have reconciled their differences. Distance has been closed, and closeness has been restored. It is this much-needed process that I hope to help you understand in this writing.

The work of repairing damaged relationships requires an understanding of certain necessary tools. Furthermore, there must be understanding of how to properly use the tools. Many people are acquainted with tools like confrontation, confession, and forgiveness, but they have used them with inadequate understanding and have thus judged the tools as inadequate. Predictably, poor use of the proper tools yields poor results. In the following pages, I will help you understand how to grasp the tools and use them properly.

CHAPTER 1

RELATIONSHIPS CAN BE CHALLENGING

You would not be reading this book if you did not already know that relationships are sometimes challenging. Surely, you also know that all relationships are not equally challenging. In fact, you probably chose to read this book with a particular relationship in mind. The tools I will encourage you to use, and guide you in their use, are applicable in any relationship that needs repair.

Our relationships are challenging because all of us humans behave poorly at times, causing disappointment, frustration, and hurt in others. In addition, we often communicate poorly, which impairs the repair process and sometimes even adds fuel to the destructive fire already ignited.

Let's start by looking at some basic facts of relationships and what it means to repair or reconcile one. There is no intent to talk down to anyone here; I simply want us to be united in our thinking as we move forward.

First, consider some dictionary definitions for the word *reconcile*. Look in any dictionary and you will find phrases like these:[1]

- To restore to friendship or harmony
- To settle or resolve differences

---

[1] (See en.wiktionary.org/wiki/reconcile, Thefreedictionary.com/reconcile, Merriam-webster.com/dictionary/reconcile)

- To restore or re-create friendly relations
- To make things compatible or consistent

Notice the unmistakable implications of these statements:

- Friendship or relational harmony once existed, but something damaged it.
- Friendly relations existed until something detrimental happened.
- A close relationship was enjoyed before a hurtful event occurred.
- A once-felt compatibility was lost in some transaction or transactions between the parties.

The process of reconciliation addresses those things that actually happened or were perceived to have happened that resulted in damage to the relationship.

The Bible draws us to consider relationships on two planes: the vertical and the horizontal. On the vertical plane is our relationship with God, our Maker and Master. On the horizontal plane are our relationships with one another. Sin has damaged relationships on both planes.

Sin? Absolutely! Sin is a biblical term, and it simply means we have failed to fulfill the will of our Maker. We may or may not have broken a law of man, but in sin we break the laws of God. Though the Bible generally advocates reconciliation, it does not do so without limits or qualifications. We will address these limitations in greater depth later; for now, I only want to acknowledge their existence.

A relationship, by definition, requires at least two parties. Where a relationship has been damaged by offense of some sort, reconciliation requires the work of both parties. This is vital truth that many people miss—that *one person cannot effect reconciliation*. I can do *my* part to reconcile, but I cannot do *your* part. Neither will God do our part. He can offer His greatest gift, but He can't make us want it or receive it. That is not to say that He does not orchestrate influential events to encourage us to receive what He has for us. He does. However, because God has endowed us with a free will, even in the face of the strongest of His influences, we must still choose to submit to Him.

In the Bible, we find a very clear explanation for all the damaged relationships in our world. We need only to read the first three chapters of the Bible to find it. The picture presented there is that of life "in the beginning." The picture is exceptionally delightful; it's almost heaven on earth. God and man enjoyed a perfect relationship; Adam and Eve had a perfect relationship; perfect peace and joy and harmony existed on planet Earth. Provision was plentiful. All was right with the world—*in the beginning*.

There was one notable difference between this "heaven on earth" situation and heaven itself. On earth was a terrible presence never tolerated in heaven—a deceiving spirit, a serpent, in that otherwise perfect garden. From these opening chapters of Genesis to the final chapters of the book of Revelation, we are made acutely aware of a spiritual war that exists between the Creator and this serpent, also known as the devil or Satan (Rev. 12:9; 20:2). That enemy of God is our enemy, too.

When we grasp the truth that we have a very real, very crafty spiritual enemy, we understand so much more about life. It helps us understand why damaged relationships are so common, and why there is so much confusion over the subject of reconciliation and related issues. The devil is an enemy who actively works to damage relationships and to *keep them* in a damaged state. He keeps us and our relationships in those damaged states by doing the following:

- Confusing us about truth
- Outright lying to us
- Leading us to believe that understanding a truth, without acting on it, is sufficient

From Adam and Eve and on through human history, Satan has worked to damage relationships between every individual and God, between one person and another. That is his core mission. We would do well to grasp this truth and respond appropriately.

Thankfully, in those opening chapters of the Bible, we also see God working to *restore* relationships. He still is. That is *His* core mission. Amazingly, He actually *wants* relationship with us—even with spiritual misfits like you and me. Furthermore, He wants us to have wholesome relationships with one another. When Jesus boiled the Bible's message down to a few words, He said, "Heaven's message comes down to these two points: love God with all you have and are, and love your neighbor as you do yourself" (Matt. 22:37–40, paraphrased). Clearly, God wants great relationships on both planes.

Many years ago, as I was reading the first of the apostle John's three epistles, I experienced a great revelation of truth. John said, "This is love for God: to obey His commands. And His commands are not burdensome" (1 John 5:3). The commands of God are not designed to be heavy burdens. They're not made to harass us or to make life more difficult; they are for our good. Whatever He asks us to do will be good. Though admittedly it might not seem good immediately, His commands will ultimately be found to be very good. When we obey, we will one day realize His command was good indeed and rejoice that we obeyed regardless of the cost, though that day of knowing may not come in this life.

We must learn to trust that God's commands are always for our good in order to learn to obey them. If God calls you to confess your sins, it is for good. If He calls you to forgive someone, it is for good. If He calls you to make restitution, it is for good. If He calls you to some very hard work, it is for good. If He calls you down a road of suffering for the sake of righteousness, it is for good. I hope you choose to trust this and obey His voice. I am certain that a hundred years from now, neither you nor I will regret any act of obedience to the Master. I firmly believe this. Do you?

Frankly, too many of us do not know or trust the truth that God is for us; thus, through either ignorance, apathy, or rebellion, we do not heed the call of God on our lives. All those damaged relationships we see and experience are a result of *someone's* failure to do the will of God. As much as possible, with the help of God, let us humbly determine not to *be* that someone.

I've already said that we can do only our part in relationships. As you read on, my intent is to equip *you* to engage in relationships in a manner that facilitates health and healing. If you take in this information and act on it, you will be able to participate in what God wants to do in your relationships and avoid cooperating with the enemy in what he wants to do in your relationships. Please note the definite call to action here. We must do certain things if we want to participate in God's work. Passivity plays well into the devil's plans. In fact, sometimes we actually participate in his destructive plans by doing nothing at all.

Do not misunderstand that point. Passivity *can* play into the hands of our enemy. Passivity and wholesome self-restraint, however, are not one and the same. Silence for the sake of ourselves and silence for the sake of others are quite different, and we must respect this fact. There are circumstances when we *should* remain silent, not speak up, not stand up, not move, not act. In the interest of strengthening, preserving, or restoring a relationship, there are certainly times to hold our tongues. A world of difference exists, however, between holding our tongues with noble purposes and merely holding our tongues because of fear and/or indifference.

Let me affirm some things you probably already know experientially. In the midst of conflict with another, restraining yourself from conveying a destructive message—with or without words—can be incredibly difficult. As a Christian, I have experienced times when I was absolutely forced to depend on the power of God to remain silent; likewise, I've found myself in other circumstances where I needed His power to speak. I have also discovered a continual need for God's wisdom to know whether to be silent or to speak. I hope you are aware of this tension, too. If this concept is foreign to you, it may be a sign that you are not taking seriously enough your God-given role in creating, maintaining, and restoring healthy relationships.

Reconciliation in relationships is necessary because of sin. If none of us ever sinned, we would never need reconciliation. If we always did God's will in our relationships, they would remain close, satisfying, and full of love. But in our sin, we often fall short of God's will in our relationships in one of two ways: either we fail to do something that God would require of us, or we do something God forbids.

The Bible could not be clearer on this point: we are all sinners. Every one of us fails by doing things we should not and not doing things we ought. Here is how the Bible describes us: "all have sinned and fall short of the glory of God" (Rom. 3:23). At times we are the one sinning, and at other times we are the one sinned against. In either case, the result is a damaged relationship. Sin always damages relationships, and because you and I are sinners (as is everyone we know), the probability of damage to our relationships is guaranteed. It is only a matter of degree.

God's will not only addresses those things that should not happen because they create offense, but it also addresses what should happen *after* those violations have occurred. When we violate God's will and offend someone else in the process, He has a will regarding what we are to do now. When someone else violates God's will and thereby offends us, He also has a will regarding what we should do now.

If we hope to help heal damaged relationships, we must take specific actions. The various components of reconciliation, the process whereby damage to relationships is effectively addressed, will direct us like a road map to specific activities appropriate in our circumstances. To do this reparative work, however, requires us to possess certain tools and to know how to use them properly. Stay with me in the following chapters and I will help you grasp and use these tools of reconciliation effectively.

CHAPTER 2

SIX CRUCIAL COMPONENTS OF RECONCILIATION

If a damaged relationship is to be restored, poor habits of relating must change. Instead of avoiding the issues, we must confront them. Instead of making excuses, we must admit wrongdoing. Instead of nursing a grudge, we must forgive. Instead of refusing to right a wrong, we must make amends. Instead of maintaining walls of distrust, we must work to remove them.

To repair a damaged relationship requires specific changes. The changes needed depend on the individuals' respective roles in the damaged relationship (the offender or the offended). Also, the degree of reconciliation sought as the ultimate goal will determine to what degree the following components of reconciliation will be utilized:

1. Confrontation
2. Confession
3. Forgiveness
4. Restitution
5. Rebuilding of trust
6. And (sometimes) acceptance

Usually, we will use all of these, but not always. Let's consider how each of these components relates to reconciliation and to one another. As we explore this subject matter, I will also attempt to clarify the exceptions to the use of all six components.

1. Confrontation

Sometimes repeated, relatively minor hurts act like a jackhammer against concrete, eventually breaking a solid relationship. Damage may also occur over a single wrong and very hurtful event. Whether relational damage results from a single major hurt or from a series of minor hurts compiled over time, the facts surrounding the hurts must be confronted if we hope to heal the damaged relationship.

Sometimes a relationship is badly damaged or even destroyed over misperceptions. Someone is offended by misinformation or a misinterpretation of facts. If hurts based on real offenses are to be distinguished from hurts based on imagined offenses, confrontation must occur between the parties. As the people in a damaged relationship communicate over the sense of offense, issues can be sorted out. Reality can be separated from misperceptions and accidental hurts separated from intentional ones. This sorting of facts must take place in order to facilitate healing and reconciliation.

So, who initiates this confrontation? Does the one who is hurt do it, or does the one who caused the hurt do it? The answer is yes on both counts. Whoever chooses the path of reconciliation first is the one who initiates confrontation over a relational hurt. If you hurt someone and are aware of the fact, you don't have to wait until the hurt person confronts you with their pain. Initiate communication over the hurt that you know or suspect you caused. On the other hand, if someone has hurt you, though they could and perhaps should approach you, you don't have to wait for that person to initiate the needed communication. You can start the difficult process.

Jesus encouraged confrontation in the eighteenth chapter of Matthew's Gospel, where He told the offended one, "Go to the offender and talk about the offense" (my paraphrase). Please notice that Jesus instructed the offended party to make the first move. In another place, however, Jesus told the offender to make the first move. Matthew recorded what could be called the "parable of an offender at worship." In this story, a man was bringing a gift to God; while at the altar, he recalled a person who had something against him. You have probably been there, with the nagging knowledge that someone is upset with you. You may or may not have known exactly what it was about. In this parable, Jesus addressed the guy who *created* the relational offense and told him to initiate the confrontation.

In telling us about the man at the altar with the premature gift, Jesus underscored how important reconciliation between humans is to God. God would happily wait on our gifts to Him while we engage in an act of greater importance in His eyes. When we become aware that we have created a rift in a relationship, Jesus expects us to make the first move to make things right.

Whoever moves first to confront the hurt in a relationship is the one most ready to be led by the God of reconciliation. When we make such a move, we can be sure He is pleased. Doing this, however, does not assure us of the desired outcome. We have no guarantees of how the other party will respond. We are only responsible for our own obedience, not that of others.

More reconciled relationships would occur if more of us would focus on our obedient relational input than on unpredictable relational outcomes. Remember, the outcome of our obedient actions is not guaranteed; that depends on the other person. Sadly, sometimes we refuse to do the right thing unless the desired outcome is certain. I encourage you, as a servant of God, to heed God's leading regardless of the outcome. Do your part and leave the results to Him.

Once confrontation has occurred, the parties should have enough shared information regarding their relational issues to facilitate further steps. Thus, they are enabled to do their respective work to reconcile and even to define the limits of that reconciliation.

Confrontation is a scary word for many of us. It sounds like something that could raise our blood pressure. The scene could get nasty. Thus, fear of confrontation leads many of us to avoid it. When we let fear lead us like this, however, we are not allowing God to guide us toward reconciliation. God will help us with our fears, if we choose to obey Him. Notice I did not say He will *remove* our fears; rather, He will help us overcome them.

Perhaps some guidance may alleviate some of your fears of confrontation and help make them more wholesome. Consider these points:

- **Speak the truth in love.** This means you should talk about the hurtful experience that damaged your relationship without doing more damage. Instead of yelling, cursing, and calling names, maintain self-control. Be clear and kind. Sarcasm and insults have no place here, though pain and anger can drive you to use them. If you can't speak without losing control, *write out* what needs to be said. This assumes that you will write something more wholesome than what you would blurt out in a moment of pain and anger. Frankly, sometimes wisdom might call you to *write* the truth in love rather than attempting to speak it.

- **Be specific.** Suppose Karen's spouse returns home from work much later than usual. For over half an hour, she has been very worried, and in the last fifteen minutes, she has been frantically calling his cell phone, which has repeatedly gone to voicemail. When she hears him come in the front door, Karen rushes to meet him there. She barks out, "About time you got home! Where have you been? Did you lose your phone?" Karen's unkind, emotionally driven statements are as unwholesome as they are understandable. They also lack the clarity to effectively address the deeper issues that exist between her and her husband. It is important to get to the deeper issues. Karen should say something like this: "I have been very worried about you for the past half hour. I feared you might have been in an accident. A phone call from you to tell me you were going to get the car serviced before you came home would have avoided all of this. I think it was very inconsiderate of you not to call. I'm hurt that you didn't do that." In this way, Karen would be specific about what caused her hurt feelings.

- **Be safe.** If you are communicating with someone prone to violent outbursts, take appropriate steps to ensure your personal safety. You might choose a public place to talk, or you could communicate by telephone. Consider having someone else present when you talk. You might even opt for written rather than verbal communication. Let me be clear: your goal here is not comfort, but safety. Confrontation may be, at best, uncomfortable; however, it need not be dangerous.

- **Be sensitive.** There is a time for everything. Confronting unacceptable and painful transactions in a relationship is difficult enough in itself; be sensitive about the timing of the communication. Try to find a time that is mutually acceptable, a time when both of you are reasonably alert and undistracted. Avoid confronting issues in front of others who have no legitimate part in the confrontation. Embarrassing the one you are confronting is counterproductive. Try to eliminate anything that would distract or derail effective communication between you and the other person.

Assuming that we intend to repair a damaged relationship, we must commit to confronting the damaging acts. Eventually, we will have to consider the work of rebuilding trust, but before we can do that, other essential work must take place. In the next section of this chapter, we will consider three core components that are necessary for repairing damaged relationships. When two people engage in these three healing actions, their work indirectly contributes to the rebuilding of trust in the relationship.

2. Confession 3. Forgiveness 4. Restitution

Let's consider the three core components involved in healing a relationship: confession, forgiveness, and restitution. We will begin with a simple scenario, though I acknowledge that most relationships do not function this simply. In a simple scenario, a relationship is damaged by one person's actions; in reality, the scenario of hurt is often not so simple, but rather, complex. We hurt each other. We have both offended and been offended. In the complex scenarios, we need to deal with both the offenses we have created *and* those from which we suffer. Nevertheless, whether simple or complex, the healing components are the same.

Let's consider now the application of these core components in a simple scenario where Andy offends his friend Ben. Andy borrowed Ben's very nice, nearly new pickup truck. He had bought some pieces of furniture from an estate sale and needed to pick them up and take them home. While doing this, however, Andy backed Ben's truck into some bushes and badly scratched the beautiful paint job. When he returned the truck, he thanked Ben for the loan of the vehicle but didn't mention the damage.

Ben didn't notice the damage until the next morning. When he saw the scratches on the body of his truck, he was first sick and then he was angry. He wanted to put some scratches on Andy's body. He vowed never to loan anything to Andy again. In fact, he didn't think he even wanted to see Andy again. Surely, you can see this relationship needs reconciliation. Again, I call the scenario simple in that Ben has done no wrong to Andy, but he strongly feels wronged by Andy.

If this relationship is to be restored, both Ben *and* Andy will have work to do. (I remind you again that we can only do our own work.) The work needed is focused on the specific acts that damaged the relationship. What damaged the relationship is related to what damaged the truck, but they are certainly separate matters. Ben must forgive Andy, and Andy will need to confess his wrongful treatment of his friend. Confession and forgiveness form the core of reconciliation. If either person refuses to do the work, reconciliation will not be achieved and the relationship will remain damaged. The damage may manifest in either open hostility or a hidden barrier of resentment. The two parties may have no relationship at all or one that no longer has significant depth.

An important question to consider at this point is this: what does Ben need to forgive, and what does Andy need to confess? To accurately answer this, we must have an accurate assessment of *what should have happened*; that is, given the circumstance, what would God have wanted to happen? At this point, we must assume some things. For instance, we have to assume that the scratches on Ben's truck are significant enough that we could reasonably conclude that Andy was aware of making them when he backed into the bush. In that case, God would have wanted Andy to return Ben's truck and say something like, "Come out here; I need to show you something. I accidentally backed into a bush and scratched your nice paint job. I am so sorry, man. Could we take it to a body shop and see what it would cost to fix it?"

When we have done wrong in a relationship—whether accidentally or purposefully—we need to confess. The biblical word *confess* means "to agree with"; that is, to agree with the truth and to agree with the one holding the truth. Biblical faith teaches us that our God is *always* holding the truth. In situations like the above scenario, we need to admit we are responsible for the deed. The truth is, we *should* be sorry that we did the deed, and that the deed resulted in loss to someone else. And, if we are in fact sorry, we should express this to the appropriate person(s).

Keep in mind that there is a very real difference between *being* sorry and merely *saying* you're sorry. Parents often work to teach their children to apologize: "Tell your brother you're sorry you broke his toy." Unfortunately, many parents fail to realize that they have only taught their children to mouth the proper words. Without question, it is far easier to teach a child to mouth the words than to adopt the attitude and feel real sorrow. Biblical confession, however, requires more than the proper words; the proper words must come from a contrite heart—and that over the wrong committed, not just from being caught or causing someone to be upset with us.

The Bible says, "Godly sorrow brings repentance" (2 Cor. 7:10). The Lord is not satisfied that we merely speak words of sorrow or present the appearance of sorrow; He wants us to *be sorrowful* over our sins. When we are truly sorry, expressing that sorrow can be powerful. When we are truly sorry, other acts will likely come to mind and be acted upon—like offering to make things right as much as we can or suggesting ways to be held accountable in the future. Remember, a sorrow that is disconnected from a turning in our hearts, an intentional internal change, is not the kind of sorrow that pleases God.

In our desired scenario above, Andy addressed another of the components of reconciliation—restitution. He suggested they get estimates on fixing the damage with the implication that he would pay for it. Restitution should be attempted in every place it is possible. Honestly, however, we can mess up some things that can never be fixed. We are all capable of doing things that we cannot undo, regardless of how desperately we and others wish it. Again, where restitution can be effected, it should be accomplished.

Let's go back and visit Ben. His nice truck is damaged. He did a good thing in loaning his truck to a friend. But his "friend" lacked the courtesy of informing him about the damage or apologizing for causing it. Backing Ben's truck into a bush damaged the truck; Andy's failure to address the issue damaged their relationship. For Ben to work on relational damage, he must first forgive Andy.

Ben does not *have to forgive* Andy, of course. He has at least one other option: he can hold on to his resentment. He can break relationship with Andy, never speak to him again, and avoid seeing him as much as possible. He can talk badly about Andy every chance he gets. Every time he gets a new scratch on his truck or anything similar, he can recall Andy and those scratches and rehearse his resentment over not being treated properly. He can even get his truck repainted and take Andy to small claims court and make him pay the bill. Even here, however, his resentment could remain. God's answer is for him to forgive the offense. *This* answer alone will rid him of the resentment.

Before we discuss more deeply this issue of forgiveness, I want to back up to that initial step we already addressed: confrontation. Remember Jesus' instructions in Matthew 18? He said, "If your brother sins against you, go and show him his fault, just between the two of you" (Matt. 18:15). Sometimes we operate with false assumptions. We assume that a person who has hurt us meant to do it and knew full well what they did. That is not always a sound assumption, however.

Here is what could happen in our scenario: After Ben discovers the damage to his truck, he goes over to Andy's place. He says something like this: "Andy, I noticed this morning some bad scratches in the paint on the back of my truck. I know those weren't there when I loaned you my truck yesterday. What happened?"

Andy might respond like this: "Oh no, really? I knew I backed into a bush when I was unloading the furniture. But I never went over to that side of the truck to see if it was damaged. I got busy unloading and forgot about it. Let's go look at it. I'm sorry; I'll do what's right by you, man."

Of course, confrontations do not always go that smoothly. You knew that, right? Andy could deny any knowledge of the damage and refuse to take any responsibility for it. He might even get angry and accuse Ben of blaming him for something he didn't do. Jesus anticipated such reactions, so He said, "If they won't listen to you, take two or three people with you and try to reason with the person" (my paraphrase of Matthew 18:16). These additional people are supposed to help with the communication. They can make sure Ben is being clear. They might challenge inconsistencies in Andy's account. Ben could get a couple of his fishing buddies (actually, a couple of his hunting buddies with their deer rifles might be more effective—just kidding here) and go talk with Andy again. Maybe Andy will hear and respond. That is the hope in Jesus' teaching.

Again, Jesus knew that this, too, would not always work, so He offered another step if the offender remains resistant to the truth: to tell it to the church. This is an admittedly hard step to take in modern America. Jesus assumes that the individuals are both part of the same church and subject to the same authority. (It might take a book the size of the Bible to line out all the possible scenarios that could exist in those situations.) One thing I believe that Jesus' teaching should mean for a believer—assuming Ben is one—is that the leaders of his church should know what is going on and become involved, minimally in prayer and probably for godly counsel. If Andy is a member of the same church, the spiritual leaders might appeal to him to respond appropriately. They might facilitate a meeting of the two men to talk through the point of conflict.

Even in the ideal situation where two people belong to the same church and are supposedly subject to the same leaders, the outcome can still be unsatisfying. Andy could stay stuck in denial and defensiveness. Jesus acknowledged this, too. If that final step fails, Jesus says, "Then treat him as a pagan or a tax collector."

Does that now mean Ben can do bodily harm to the ex-friend? Can he go "key" Andy's car to get even? Absolutely not! It does mean they will no longer be close friends. Whatever dealings they have will be those of necessity. Think of what Jesus said. If the tax man comes to me, I will give him my taxes and that is it. I won't ask him to come in for dinner. We won't be going fishing together on a weekend. We will not have a close relationship. Our relationship will be limited to the necessary; anything unnecessary will be unacceptable.

Reconciliation is not without limits. I want us to think about this statement together. We cannot expect that all relationships will be restored to the same condition enjoyed prior to a serious injury. This reality is related to the violation of trust that damaged the relationship. Though God calls us to forgive all offenses committed against us, He does not expect us to fully trust people who have

Six Crucial Components Of Reconciliation

violated our trust in major ways. Consider this poignant example: If a family member molested one of my children, I would need to do the extremely hard work of forgiving the molester in order to rid my heart of bitterness and hatred and vindictiveness. I would hope, at some point, to be capable of being civil at necessary family social functions. But *never* again would that family member be trusted alone with any children with whom I have influence. Definite limits would exist in our reconciliation. The trust that I once had would surely never be restored. Even my socializing with the molester would be limited to absolutely necessary situations.

Consider another example with me. Suppose my best friend and my wife engaged in some grossly inappropriate communication with each other. I discovered the emails and text messages between them. Physical cheating had not happened as far as I could tell, but emotional cheating was undeniable. Would not my relationship with both of them be terribly damaged? Fortunately, nothing like this has ever happened to me, and I cannot imagine that it ever would. However, I have counseled many couples caught in this very situation. Often the betrayed spouse chooses as I imagine I would: he engages in the hard work to save his marriage but ends the close friendship. Thus, there is the choice to reconcile one relationship and not the other.

For more biblical evidence that we are not to be reconciled to everyone, consider Paul's instructions in Second Timothy. Here he talks about people who appear to be religious but are clearly "lovers of self and lovers of pleasure more than lovers of God," and he states emphatically, "Have nothing to do with them" (2 Tim. 3:5). Again, in his letter to Titus regarding a divisive person in the church, Paul instructs, "Warn a divisive person once, and then warn him a second time. After that, have nothing to do with him" (Titus 3:10). These are not pictures of reconciled relationships.

One final piece of evidence should prove that reconciliation is not always the goal in damaged relationships. The evidence relates to that very special relationship called marriage. When a man and a woman enter marriage by personal choice, we can safely assume that a state of closeness generally exists. However, that closeness can be damaged by many things. In fact, it can become so badly damaged that God does not expect a person to reconcile the relationship. Divorce, for example, is recognized by almost everyone as an acceptable option under one condition—adultery. When this painful experience occurs in this unique relationship, God grants the violated one an exemption from their marital vows. The violated one need not feel obliged to maintain the marriage.

It is important to remember that this is *an allowance* of the Holy One, not a command. Thus, in a marriage where one partner has cheated, the other can choose whether or not to do the hard work of reconciliation. Many people do choose the hard work, but God does not demand it. The fact that God does not require reconciliation in this relationship, where vows to love "till death do us part" are typically expressed, should convince anyone that God does not require full reconciliation in all relationships and in all circumstances.

Reconciliation certainly has legitimate limits. Relational offenses damage and sometimes destroy trust between people. The degree of damage to trust directly relates to two factors:

1. The degree of reconciliation that will take place in a relationship

2. The time required to effect that reconciliation

Sometimes the damage to trust is so great that there will be *no* reconciliation. This is the issue behind adultery, the one indisputable biblical justification for divorce. When a marital partner has committed adultery—a most grievous breach of trust—the God of reconciliation does not require reconciliation. On the other hand, neither does He require divorce; He merely allows it in His graciousness. The existence of that allowance, however, provides unquestionable evidence that God endorses some limits to reconciliation.

Given that limits to reconciliation do exist, we nonetheless ought to pursue reconciliation as close to those limits as possible.

Just because reconciliation is difficult work does not mean we should not engage in it with passion.

Let's briefly return to the subject of confrontation. Is there any reason to confront an issue with someone with whom you have no intention of reconciling? Even in a relationship where you may legitimately choose not to reconcile, the facts regarding that choice should generally be communicated in some manner. Go back to my illustration of discovering inappropriate communication between a best friend and my spouse. I should not merely cut off communication with my old friend (stop calling him and ignore his calls); rather, I should, in some wholesome manner, communicate that our friendship is over and tell him why. He should be aware that I have found the emails, feel betrayed by him, and want nothing more to do with him. That would be fitting confrontation.

If We Aren't Going to Be Reconciled...

We have been considering reconciliation and components of this process. We have shown that reconciliation is not a legitimate goal in every damaged relationship. Two obvious questions arise: If we are not going to reconcile with someone, do we still need to forgive? Or, if we are sure the person we have offended will never choose to reconcile with us, is there any point in confessing our sin or attempting to make restitution? As a matter of fact, in both these situations there *is* still a need to forgive, confess wrongdoing, and make whatever restitution is possible.

The components of reconciliation have purposes in addition to the restoration of the wounded relationships. They enable the hearts of the wounded individuals to heal. Of course, if a relationship is to heal, the hearts wounded by the offenses need to heal. Those hearts need restoration even if the relationship is not restored. Failure to understand and appreciate this truth has created much confusion, even among Christians.

Let's consider another example in order to illustrate the operation of reconciliation principles wherein reconciliation of the relationship is not the goal. Bill and Cheryl had been married almost nine years when Cheryl discovered that Bill had been cheating on her with her close friend Kaylene. They had been cheating on their spouses for almost two years. It was Kaylene's husband, Dave, who discovered the affair and informed Cheryl.

When Dave first told Cheryl, she thought it must be a sick joke. However, he assured her that he had proof and had already confronted Kaylene with the irrefutable evidence. Initially, she had tried to deny everything, but finally, she admitted it. Cheryl had never felt so devastated by anything in her entire life. She sank into a season of deep depression during which merely taking care of her two children was almost more than she could accomplish. She had never thought that Kaylene would betray her like this, and it had been utterly unthinkable that Bill would do this to her.

Cheryl and Bill separated immediately. Through the six months of deep depression that followed the revelation of the affair, Cheryl had no energy to work on her relationship with Bill. She went to counseling, mostly to deal with the debilitating depression that nearly wiped out her joy and sometimes threatened even her desire to live. She told her counselor that she felt as if her whole marriage had been a lie, not just the last two years, which had certainly been a lie. Having been blasted by a double-barreled betrayal, she didn't know if she could ever trust anyone again. She certainly couldn't trust Bill again.

About a year after the exposé, Cheryl filed for divorce. Dave and Kaylene had engaged in counseling and appeared to be working things out. This information came to Cheryl through mutual friends. Cheryl, however, would not attempt to reconcile with Bill.

Let's return to the questions already raised: If Cheryl is not going to reconcile with Bill, does she need to forgive him? When Bill learns that Cheryl is not open to reconciliation, does he still need to confess his sin? It is my deeply held conviction that God would want both of them to take these personal steps for their own merit, not just as components of reconciliation. Again, forgiveness and confession are acts that facilitate healing of individuals, not just reconciliation in relationships. Even when reconciliation is not an option, healing is. Though a relationship may never be restored, the parties in that relationship can be. This is the will of God.

Understanding Forgiveness

Maybe you know what it means to forgive, or maybe not. Nevertheless, let's take a moment to walk through this. What does it mean to forgive? The biblical word means to cancel a debt. When we are mistreated, we incur a relational debt; that is, we are owed something that has not been paid. We could be owed something tangible like money, but often it is something intangible like honesty, honor, respect, or fidelity. Regardless of the particulars, we are called to forgive whenever and wherever we have been mistreated. Before we can cancel a debt, however, we must first identify the debt to be cancelled; and once we have accurately identified the debt (what was owed, what was lost), we must make the choice to cancel it. This is forgiveness.

If Cheryl wants her heart to heal, the debt related to Bill's infidelity must be dealt with effectively. Forgiveness is the medicine that will heal her heart. In fact, forgiveness is the *only* medicine that will heal such a heart. Without this God-prescribed medicine, her heart will become home to resentment and bitterness, and to some degree this will steal her joy and impair her ability to love and be loved.

Honestly, sometimes it seems rational to hold on to debts. We reason, *Someone has to pay. I deserve it. I can't go on without this being settled.* These statements are true. Someone has to pay—Jesus did. We do deserve to be treated fairly—but none of us are. The debt does need to be settled—but this settling is sometimes accomplished only via forgiveness. Forgiveness is a choice to cancel the real debt, accept the associated loss, and choose to believe that our God can lead us into blessing in spite of that loss.

So, even though Cheryl intends never to reconcile with Bill, she needs to forgive his monumental violation against her. In her heart, she must cancel the debt that Bill owes her, which is as huge as it is legitimate. This act, as with every act of forgiveness, primarily works for the benefit of the one who is forgiving. It primarily effects healing in the heart of the wounded one.

In my many years of counseling, I have encountered many people who have never done this work and instead carry their wounded heart into marriage. Sometimes their heart was wounded in their childhood home, and sometimes their heart was wounded in a first marriage. You can probably guess what happens in either case. After the euphoria of a new romantic relationship fades, the bitterness of the wounded heart begins to surface. Destructive transactions begin to grow in the new relationship. Join together in holy matrimony two people with these unresolved wounds of the heart, and you have a recipe for serious marriage problems.

Have you ever wondered why we have such a high divorce rate? Furthermore, have you ever considered that many of the marriages among the half that don't divorce are not especially healthy or satisfying? Long before divorce became common in America, dysfunctional marriages were very common. Many deteriorated marriage relationships result from unresolved sin in the lives of marital partners. Sometimes the deterioration is predominantly a result of offenses that happened in the marriage. Often, however, the deterioration is a result of offenses in the marriage piled on top of unresolved offenses one or both partners brought into the marriage. These can be injurious issues from a previous marriage, other romantic relationships, a friendship, or from the family of origin. We cannot have healthy relationships unless our hearts are healthy, and trying to *act* healthy is not sufficient. Furthermore, denying the effects of sin on our hearts never facilitates the healing needed. We must use the medicine of confession and forgiveness.

Let's turn our attention back to Bill. Cheryl wants no more to do with him; she made that abundantly clear up to and throughout their divorce proceedings. Let's suppose that Bill made some initial gestures of confession and apology. Once he discovered that Cheryl didn't want to hear his words or attempt to restore their relationship, it might seem completely reasonable to many of us that he should forget the confession part. However, that would be to hold an unwholesomely narrow view of the function of confession.

Confession *is* an integral part of relational reconciliation, but it has value apart from that. Confession has personal value. When we have hurt someone else with our sin, God wants us to confess that sin. In some way, this is essential to the healing of our heart. It is not only important that the one who suffered as a result of our sin hears our words of confession; it is also important to our heart that we speak them.

Remember, to confess means to agree with the truth in our situation. We agree with the one we offended to the degree that they are holding truth. Sometimes, however, wounded people hold some things other than the truth, and we are under no obligation to agree with them in these things.

True confession is more than an admission of an act. It is that, of course, but it is so much more. It is to confess that we did something we should not have done or didn't do something we should have done, and that we were wrong in this. It is to acknowledge that we owed someone better treatment. In cases where the debt cannot be paid—for example, Bill cannot undo his infidelity—an appeal for forgiveness and a chance to prove sorrow over the sin are all that can be done. And this should be offered.

Just as we saw that Cheryl did not have to forgive, neither does Bill have to confess. He has options, too. This is predictable, friends; wherever we find the will of God, we will always find options to the contrary. Bill can refuse to take responsibility for his actions.

He can blame others. He can minimize what he did and try to make excuses for it, but if he does these things, he will inflict wounds upon his own heart that will undoubtedly show up later in some destructive form or another. He may never recognize this, but the One who sees all will see. He wants Bill to be honest about his sin, and He wants that of you and me. This is the essence of confession—being honest with ourselves, with God, and with others.

In Bill's case, confessing his sin against Cheryl to her may not be feasible. She may not be willing to talk at all; she might even have a restraining order in place. Even if she is absolutely unreceptive, he can still confess (agree with the truth). He can exercise this honesty within himself; he can confess to God and to another human being his sins that wounded Cheryl, Dave, and others. This would provide a healing balm to Bill's heart. Scripture instructs us most clearly on this issue, saying, "Confess your sins to each other and pray for each other so that you may be healed" (Jas. 5:16). Notice that the context of this passage is not reconciliation of a relationship, but rather healing of individuals.

I hope it is clear that forgiveness and confession are to be chosen even when reconciliation is not the goal. Forgiveness resolves the injury to the heart of the one offended. Initially, to forgive says, "I know that the way I was treated was wrong, even if the one who treated me thusly never sees it." Having recognized a legitimate relational debt, the call for forgiveness then requires us to cancel the debt stored in our heart. Likewise, confession resolves the injury to the heart of the offender. True confession is, at its core, an act of a heart honestly convicted of wrongdoing; it is more than to acquiesce to the accusations of an offended person.

Besides the personal effects of each of these acts, they also facilitate reconciliation of the relationship where that is chosen by the parties, and that is normally God's goal. Reconciliation is what He would want ideally. In His relationship with us, God wants reconciliation, but not without conditions. The apostle Peter described God's disposition toward us as sinners, saying, "He is patient with you, not wanting anyone to perish, but everyone to come to repentance" (2 Pet. 3:9b). Of course, not everyone comes to repentance in order to be reconciled to God. Though He does not want anyone to perish, many will. However, this will be the result of the stubbornness of their hearts, not the unwillingness of His.

I hope this explanation helps you see how these various elements work in our lives and relationships where sin has caused damage. Before I wrap this up, I want to emphasize that each party on both sides of an offense has specific work to do. The offended one needs to forgive, and the offender needs to confess. These independent acts create healing in the individuals involved and offer an opportunity for reconciliation in the relationship.

Let's suppose that an offense has severely damaged a relationship. Let's further suppose that the two parties have confronted the offense, and each has acted in the scripturally prescribed manner; that is, the offender has confessed the wrong and the offended one has forgiven. The offender has received forgiveness and cleansing from God and has received an expression of forgiveness from the person offended. The offended one has forgiven the offender and is trusting God with that which was lost in the violation. As a result, they are both at peace in their hearts. But, is all well relationally? Not necessarily! We have another important component of reconciliation to look at—the rebuilding of trust.

5. Rebuilding Damaged Trust

When an offense has damaged a relationship, part of what is damaged is the trust between the two parties. For full reconciliation to be accomplished, this trust must be rebuilt. Because all offenses are not alike, they do not damage trust equally. Some minor offenses create minor dings to trust, while some other offenses can wipe out trust completely. Damage to trust in relationships lies on a continuum from very minor dings to absolute annihilation.

How is trust rebuilt? The offender must "produce fruit in keeping with repentance" (Matt. 3:8). That quotation is from John the Baptist in his ministry of preaching repentance to the Jews. He wanted the people to know that the repentance God desires is not in name or theory alone, but a genuine repentance, a true turning of the heart that is manifested in new choices and new behaviors. When we really turn, or change our minds (the core meaning of repentance), it produces different fruit—fruit that indicates we have truly made the right turn. Thus, when we have treated someone with sinful disregard, the fruit of repentance necessary to the rebuilding of trust is a new pattern of wholesome consideration in our relationship with the person we previously harmed by our sin.

The task of rebuilding trust is different in every situation. The magnitude of the task is directly related to the magnitude *and* the frequency of the offense. For instance, if I have treated my wife harshly on an almost daily basis for years, she might begin to really trust my repentance after a few months of no harsh treatment. Notice I said "begin." We naturally build walls to protect our hearts in the face of threat; those walls do not come down easily or quickly. Even after a fairly long season of the offensive treatment being extinguished, many people will continue to be emotionally on guard.

Suppose, however, I am now harsh once every week or two. Can you see that the rebuilding of trust will be substantially slowed? My occasional harshness tells my wife that my repentance is not a secured state; therefore, she is not secure in our relationship. Hate this, if you must; but if you intend to rebuild trust where you have broken it, you will need to embrace this reality.

It is precisely at this point of rebuilding trust after repentance that many of us fail. We repent of our bad behavior for a while; but then, we repent of our repentance and go back to our old sinful ways. In this situation, the offended party cannot redevelop trust. I have encountered many marital relationships where one partner has practiced this pattern for so long that their earnest, expressed intent to "really change this time" is met with "yeah, right." The couple's history includes serial fights over some poor treatment. The fights were resolved by the offender promising to change. And he or she did change—for a few days, a few weeks, even a few months. However, the pattern remains the same in that the bad behavior eventually returns and stays—until the one suffering has had enough, again.

In these situations, I have encouraged many of these men and women to finally, genuinely repent—to stay the course in their repentance with the hope that it will someday be believed and trusted. I always warn them that they will have to go much longer than they have ever gone before on the road of repentance. Unknowingly, they have taught the other person to trust this: "It will only be a matter of time until I start treating you badly again." Not until that lesson is replaced with "You can trust me; I have really changed" will full reconciliation be possible. In those instances, I have seen relationships restored after horrific violations of trust as an offender took seriously the task of rebuilding trust, and the offended one assumed the risks inherent to trusting again.

Trust has to do with boundaries. When rebuilding trust, we may think the logical goal is to restore previous boundaries. That is not always the case, however. For instance, if a family member did something sexually inappropriate with my child (or any child for that matter), I would never restore the previous boundary of trust. If I trusted the offender's repentance, I might allow him to be around my children again, but *never again alone*. This example is admittedly extreme but serves my purpose well. Complete restoration of trust is not always an appropriate goal. Seek godly counsel if you question your motives in placing limits on the restoration of trust (are my limits appropriate, or am I being vindictive?).

Now, let's consider one more important issue.

6. Acceptance

The late Amy Carmichael, missionary to India in the twentieth century, wrote a poem entitled "In Acceptance Lieth Peace." The stanzas proclaim that peace comes not in forgetting, nor in human endeavor, aloofness, or submission, but rather "in *acceptance* lieth peace." Of course, there is a legitimate place and function for forgetting and for human endeavor, submission, and even aloofness; but Amy suggests there is a kind of peace found only in acceptance. I believe she is right.

I cannot leave the subject of restoring damaged relationships without addressing this powerful key of *acceptance*. Sometimes confession and forgiveness are *not* the powerful keys needed to mend a relationship. Those two actions concern real offenses committed in a relationship. The hurts we experience sometimes fall outside this common area; that is, sometimes a real offense is not the source of our pain and guardedness, but rather the perception (or more accurately, misperception) of an offense.

Maybe you have held a grudge against your parents for years because they did not have the financial resources to provide some things you really wanted, things many of your peers received from their parents. You may have even carried a grudge against God over this experience. I hope you know, as an adult, that neither your parents nor God owed you the finest in current fashion apparel. Kids can be cruel, to be sure; they can make other kids who come to school wearing off-brand shoes, shirts, or jeans feel worthless. A real offense may need to be settled with those kids who made fun of you. If your parents, however, provided according to their ability, your sense of offense is not settled by forgiving your parents for not bedecking you better. The real solution lies in acceptance.

Amy Carmichael recognized a very important truth. To move to the place of acceptance is a heart-changing move. It empowers us to settle something that otherwise would remain unsettled in us. You can accept a disappointing reality without denying the disappointment of it. You can accept the limited resources of your family without needing to blame someone or be resentful for those limits. You don't need to go through life feeling that you have somehow been short-changed or ripped off. Indeed, in acceptance lieth peace—*your peace*.

Life offers an abundance of disappointing experiences where no one has actually sinned, done wrong to us, or intentionally withheld good from us. Our hurt feelings can simply be a result of not getting our way or of having an unpleasant experience. Losses, for example, are common unpleasant experiences, and losses vary in intensity from mild to devastating. Sometimes these losses are a result of innocent actions. If Mom or Dad is promoted in his/her company, and the deal requires a move to a different city in another state, you may, as a child, suffer the loss of relationship. Your very best friend will not be moving with you. This can be a very great and painful loss. Furthermore, you may find it difficult to adjust to a new community.

To "forgive" Mom or Dad for moving the family is not really the solution; grieving the loss to the point of acceptance is the true solution. When such losses happen to children, they do not always resolve the matters of the heart. They may live with a level of resentment that is generally hidden from sight. The good news is as an adult, you can look back at experiences where acceptance was missed and choose to move there now. Doing so can bring peace to an area of your heart in need of it. And that peace can positively affect relationships in your life.

Summarizing the Material Thus Far

In a relationship damaged by sin, we are on one side or the other of the sin. We either committed the offense or we suffered as a result of the offense. It is not unusual that this process is complex; that is, we have been offended *and* we have offended. Complex sin processes can be broken down into simple transactions, where each party takes responsibility for his or her own part in damaging the relationship. Each person can confess the wrong done. Each one can confront the wrong suffered. The offender can choose to obey God, honestly confessing the wrong. If the offender can make meaningful restitution, this should be done. The offended one can choose to obey God by grace and forgive. Both the offender and offended must then work on rebuilding trust.

However, there are some problems associated with this process. That is our next issue to examine.

CHAPTER 3

THREE PROBLEMS RELATED TO THE RECONCILIATION PROCESS

I have already stated that we have options concerning each component of reconciliation. Instead of forgiving, we can hold on to our resentments until we feel we have gotten even, which will probably be never. Instead of confessing, we can engage in a variety of other acts like blaming others, making excuses, and making light of our wrongdoing. In this chapter, we will consider three other problems associated with the process of reconciliation. They are sinful confrontations, faulty confessions, and faulty forgiveness.

1. Sinful Confrontations

When we have been hurt by someone else's wrongdoing, we can let that hurt drive us to confront the offender in a hurtful way. We can attack the person, not just address the sinful actions, and feel totally justified in our attack. It is absolutely true that violations can leave us not only hurt but also very angry, and anger can drive us to sinful behaviors in all sorts of circumstances. Scripture, therefore, instructs us thusly: "In your anger do not sin" (Eph. 4:26). When we fail to abide by this admonition, we will sin in our attempt to confront someone else's sin.

If in your attempts to confront wrong behavior in others, you have let your anger drive you to do so in a mean and/or abusive manner, you should confess this and ask for forgiveness. If you have been confronted in such an abusive manner, you should confront the confronter, although not necessarily at the moment when the person is obviously upset with you. This confrontation should not be an attempt to deflect attention from the original purpose of the confrontation, because your first responsibility is to respond to that.

Suppose your spouse asked you to run an errand on the way home from work (pick something up from the grocery store or the dry cleaners). You agreed to do this but then forgot. When your spouse sees you at home and you don't have what was requested, you are attacked in anger: "I knew I couldn't count on you. You are absolutely worthless. You make me sick! I'll never ask you to do anything for me again." For the rest of that evening and the next day—and maybe a few more days—you are treated with contempt for your offense.

Yes, that is wrong. It is offensive, too.

What I am about to say may be hard to hear; it will probably be even harder to do. Your initial response to your spouse should not be a defensive confrontation of their attack on your person. Rather, it should be something like this: "Dear, I am truly sorry that I forgot to do what you asked. It was thoughtless of me, and I get it that you are very hurt by this. You certainly have a right to be hurt."

If it is possible to fix the problem (go to the grocery store and get milk), by all means, do so. But if you can't fix the problem (the cleaners is closed by now), then offer to help in any way you can. Now, do you *feel* like doing that after you have been attacked in the way I described above? Well, not if you're anything like me. Frankly, your feelings do not matter. You were irresponsible. You let down someone you love. You broke your word. Your spouse's hurt feelings are justified—not necessarily the degree of the feelings, but certainly having hurt feelings in such circumstances. Your first job, therefore, is to validate those feelings. Remember, you do not need to validate the *level* of the feelings; just validate the essence of the feelings and the real source.

After you have validated the hurt caused by your irresponsible behavior, you can address the hurtful way in which you were confronted. Sometimes that can be done immediately. Usually, it is best to wait until the upset person has calmed down. Actually, after a transaction like the one I described, you may need to wait until both of you have calmed down. When you do confront the hurtful confrontation, you should again affirm that what you did was wrong, that you let the other person down. Then you can say something like, "When you confronted me about that, I felt attacked. You said things to me that were very hurtful. I remember you called me worthless. That's not fair. It's not right."

In some cases, this could be an opportunity to start a new fight. Be prepared for that. Your spouse might shoot back something like, "Yeah, like you always talk nice to me when you're upset. You're such a jerk!" If you are prepared for this possibility, you can decline the invitation to a new fight. You can simply reply, "I don't want to fight about this; I just told you what I needed to say about your behavior." Then leave it there. You may need to physically leave the room or the building, but *do not argue the point*. You can peaceably discuss the point, but do not argue. I trust you know the difference between a discussion and an argument. When an argument breaks out, communication breaks down. In an argument, people tend to listen only in order to formulate their response. Please avoid this.

Many of us lose it at this very point. We say something to someone that they don't want to hear—a truth that is hard for them to accept. They choose to defend themselves. They counterattack. Then we engage in a long argument with them over this. By the time the argument is finished, the other person has probably forgotten the truth you originally intended to present. It has been buried under a pile of angry words, the debris of strife. If you want to deal with damaging transactions in a relationship, you must confront things that have damaged it, and you must do this in a healthy manner.

2. Faulty Confessions

The next problem is faulty confessions. When we attempt to confess our wrongs, we must avoid lacing the confession with self-protective statements. Reasons should not be presented as excuses. Sometimes it is appropriate to explain to someone why we did what we did or failed to do what we should have done. Nonetheless, we must not allow our reasons to become excuses.

This is especially true where our sinful action is closely related to that of the other party. For example, we sometimes say, "I was wrong to _____, but you _____!" The net result is a one-third confession. It is one-third confession, one-third confrontation, and one-third justification. Only full confessions, however, have healing power. If you have a habit of making these ineffective confessions, you can fix this rather easily—at least in theory. If you become aware of the fact that you offered a confession that was less than full, you can go back and make it right with the right words and a right attitude of heart.

Vague confessions are impotent, too. "I'm sorry if I did something that hurt you" often only means "I'm sorry you are upset with me," not "I'm sorry I did something that upset you." If you honestly don't know what you did to upset someone, ask them to explain it to you, but please don't ask unless you are genuinely interested in hearing and doing your part to repair the relationship.

The worst thing about these inadequate confessions is not that they are ineffective, but that they leave the one making the confession with the impression that they have done that which is right and needed. If you want your confession to have healing power for both you and the one you have hurt, you must communicate honestly and contritely—heart to heart. It can be helpful to communicate your confession repeatedly when serious breaches are the issue. An initial expression of confession is often laced with self-defense—sometimes heavily so. A second expression of wrongdoing and sorrow can be considerably less laden with self-defensive elements. A third or fourth or fifth might be completely free of these contaminants.

3. Faulty Forgiveness

The final problem is faulty forgiveness. Entire books have been written on the subject of forgiveness. Most of us readily acknowledge that we should forgive in situations where we have been wronged and hurt by others. We know that forgiveness is the answer, and therein lies a big problem. Let me explain.

When you studied math in elementary school, your teacher surely gave you homework and tests with problems to solve. Whether multiplication, division, or some other function, the teacher likely instructed you to show your work. Why was that? The teacher wanted to know that you knew how to reach the answer, not just what the answer was. You could use a calculator or look on someone else's paper to get the answer, but that is no substitute for knowing how to work the problem to arrive at the correct answer. This is the problem many of us have with the issue of forgiveness. We know that forgiveness is the answer, but we are clueless on how to move from our real problem with the offense to that true answer.

When people know that forgiveness is the answer but don't really know how to do the work involved in moving to the legitimate answer, they tend to do something that they label as forgiveness but actually is not. It is forgiveness in name only, not in substance. To merely say the words, as appropriate as that is, is not the same as doing the work of forgiveness in our hearts. We must recognize and cancel the debt we hold in our hearts. After we have done this work, we can speak from our hearts, with meaning and power, those appropriate words "I forgive you."

I must add one more possibility to the above scenario. Sometimes the problem is not one of ignorance of how to do the work involved; to the contrary, it is to know very well how hard that work can be and choosing instead to take a shortcut. We choose to merely apply the correct answer via use of the correct words, thus appearing to others that we have actually done the difficult work of forgiving. It is even possible to be self-deceived in this so that we imagine to have actually forgiven a great debt when, in fact, the debt is still fully held in the heart, though perhaps completely hidden. I suppose the psalmist was considering this very human potential when he prayed, "Search me, O God, and know my heart; test me and know my anxious thoughts. See if there is any offensive way in me, and lead me in the way everlasting" (Ps. 139:23–24). We are wise to pray this prayer often that we might see what God sees.

It is not simple work to recognize and cancel debts in relationships. Sometimes we find it easier to rationalize the offense. Canceling the debt caused by sin is not the same as making excuses for the debt, rationalizing the offense. I have heard, for instance, many people raised by an abusive parent (like my father) who say, "Well, he had a bad childhood himself. He never learned how to be a good dad." Such statements address a valid point. Though a person may have had an abusive, unloving childhood experience, they are not freed from the constraints of moral law. I have come to understand some of the formative influences on my father and have compassion on him for those; still, I had to forgive him for his failures as a father. He owed me and others a debt that was never paid. We can understand why someone does something wrong without excusing them for the choice to do wrong. This is the task of true forgiveness.

Finally, on this point of problems related to forgiveness, let's consider another difficult, yet serious, matter. Forgiveness may be needed even when no sense of offense exists. This is some of the most difficult work I encounter as a counselor. Consider this: Alan was raised by quite ineffective parents. As a child, he was not given proper parental restrictions. Dad was not around much, and when he was, he exerted no disciplinary influence. Mom was the only engaged parent, and she was very permissive. They let him do whatever he wanted, gave him whatever he asked for—or in some cases, whatever he threw a fit for. Alan was what some call a "spoiled brat." Eventually, however, we all grow up (or at least we get older).

As an adult living a very self-centered life in a series of dysfunctional relationships, Alan might have great difficulty realizing that his parents owed him better treatment and that a need to forgive them exists. When asked about his childhood, he might say it was great and that he was the luckiest kid in the neighborhood. But was he really fortunate to have been left to his own devices? If Alan ever realizes the parental failures and decides to forgive them, it may be a purely cognitive and spiritual exercise. His emotions may never register the offenses that he could, with the help of the Spirit of truth, come to understand as offenses and actually forgive.

CHAPTER 4
CLOSING THOUGHTS

Realizing That Two Parties Are Involved

Because we are all imperfect creatures, we do things that damage our relationships, and either by action or inaction, we do things that perpetuate the damage. God, therefore, expects all of us to do our part in repairing damaged relationships. He wants us to be skilled at confessing our sins and forgiving offenses, and learn when, where, and how to rebuild trust in damaged relationships. This is why I titled my book *Everyone's Job—Repairing Damaged Relationships*. Damaging relationships is what everyone does; trying to repair them, then, is what everyone is supposed to do.

By definition, a relationship involves two parties. Both parties bear responsibility for the state of the relationship. In every one of your damaged relationships, you are one party. God intends that you shoulder only *your* responsibility in the relationship. Though one person can effectively destroy a relationship, one person cannot heal or restore a relationship.

In Scripture we find this pertinent word: "If it is possible, as far as it depends on you, live at peace with everyone" (Rom. 12:18). Notice that important phrase in the middle, "as far as it depends on you." However, it *doesn't* all depend on you. You may do your part, but that does not ensure that the other party will do their part. Do your part anyway. You may have to do your part with the realization that the goal you hope for, a restored relationship, may never be realized. In that instance, it can help to keep your focus on a different goal—obedience to the Lord of relationships. In so doing, you may not reach your goal, but you will reach His goal for you.

Checking Your Motives

Why we do things is at least as important as what we do. I encourage you to do things simply because you are convinced that they are the right things to do. Do them as acts of obedience to God. Place the results in His hands, and place yourself in His hands. Resist doing things in relationships in order to manipulate (*I'll do what I should so you'll do what you should*). Beware of the effect of sinful pride that would have you do right things to impress others or be viewed favorably by others (*See what a good person I am? I'm better than you; I made the first move*).

Dealing with Repeated Offenses

What if someone in your life keeps offending in the same way over and over? Do you simply accept apology after apology? Do you just keep on forgiving and forgiving? Is that it? In situations like this, one of two things probably needs to be done. First, you may need to enlist the help of a counselor to explore factors that may be feeding a repetitive cycle of irritation. Second, you might need to make an agreement with each other about an incentive to help the offender change behavior.

I'll illustrate this point with an example from a couple I know who actually resolved such a repetitive, irritating pattern in their relationship. The husband was a professional man and the sole wage earner in the household. The wife was the typical stay-at-home mom raising the kids and taking care of domestic issues. They operated with a budget, and the husband did most of the bill paying, financial documentation, and financial management. He gave his wife a certain amount of money from his paychecks on the first and fifteenth of the month to cover food and the other household expenses for which she was responsible.

An irritating pattern developed where almost every payday the wife had to approach her husband and request the money she needed. His stated reason for the repeated breach was "I forgot." He was always happy to give her the money when he was reminded, and he felt no offense at being asked, but the wife felt a growing sense of offense as months rolled on with this pattern in place.

Finally, they had a confrontation about this, and in the process, they made an agreement: On any payday where the husband failed within five days to give his wife the money she needed to run the household, thus causing her to have to request the money, he would give her an additional fifty dollars to do with as she pleased. After making this agreement, he rarely forgot to give her the money. Having to fork out extra cash was a workable reminder for him to be faithful to the agreement. On the rare occasion that he did forget, his wife was not nearly as irritated, now having some extra cash to splurge on something. This type of agreement can work if both parties will agree that the painful pattern needs to end and if a mutually acceptable penalty for failure to perform can be found.

Forgiving on Two Relational Planes

Relationships exist on two planes: between God and ourselves, and ourselves and other human beings. Restoration of relationships is needed on both planes. Though our theology may be pure enough to hold that God never does anything wrong in relationship with us, we can nonetheless *feel* wronged by Him. I have. Life experience can take us into some very disturbing places.

I think of people who have had godly loved ones die in awful ways. Job's experience comes to mind. He felt punished by God and was confident that he didn't deserve it. The opening chapter of the book assures us that Job's assessment was partially correct. He didn't deserve the incredible upheaval to his life. However, God was not punishing him.

It is possible to be angry with God, like Job was, because He has allowed some grossly unfair event to happen. Though technically God does not need our forgiveness—in that God does not do any wrong that He should be forgiven—a forgiveness-like act is needed on our part. We need to release the anger, resentment, and bitterness we carry toward Him over the sense of offense we have experienced. We can honestly express our disappointment to God, our confusion over our experience, and our desire to lay these things down and trust again. We can enlist His help. He understands our painful experiences better than we do, and He can handle our honest communication about them.

Accepting Help

God made us for relationships. He knows all about them. He will help us build them wisely and enable us to repair them when needed. Invite Him to help you.

God has called some of us to work with Him in this important endeavor. It is often wise to engage the help of a pastor or Christian counselor when you are struggling with damaged relationships. A pair of trained and unbiased eyes and ears can be a valuable asset in these situations. With help, you just might get somewhere that you cannot achieve on your own. I've seen it happen many times, and from both chairs—the one needing the help and the one giving the help. May the God of relationships, the God of reconciliation, bless you greatly as you seek His will and His way.

Personal Application

We have thought through this important subject together. Now it is time to make personal application. To that end, write out your response to the following questions:

1. On which of the two relational planes do you have relationships that are in need of repair? Horizontal, vertical, or both?

Name the person(s) with whom you have a damaged relationship.

2. Which principle of repairing relationships is most challenging to you, and why?

3. In which of your relationships does the damage remain because you have not been willing to do your part? Be honest.

4. In which of your relationships does damage remain because the other person has not been willing to do his/her part?

5. Have you asked God to show you how you have damaged relationships by your actions or inactions? If you have not done this, would you do it now? (Don't ask if you really don't want to know. If you do want to know, don't ask just once. Ask and keep on asking in earnest!)

6. Have you made inadequate attempts to confess wrongdoing to another? How was it inadequate? Would you try to communicate again? (Set a deadline. Enlist someone to hold you accountable for following through.)

7. Where do you suspect you have fallen short in truly forgiving offenses against you? Why do you think this is true?

8. How has disappointment with God been a factor in impairing you to either confess or forgive sins?

9. Provide an example of acceptance being applied in your life. Where might it need to be applied?

ADDENDUM

BE RECONCILED TO GOD

I wrote the message of this book primarily with our human relationships in mind, though I have drawn attention to relationships on two planes. I assumed that most people who choose to read *Everyone's Job—Repairing Damaged Relationships* would be doing so because of recognized damaged relationships on the human plane. I also wrote with an assumption that may not be true for all my readers: I assumed that they were reconciled to God.

In the event that you are not sure if that is true for you, I have added this section. I want you to be reconciled with God. I want you to be sure you are. Reconciliation with God was a passion of Christ's apostles and is an abiding passion of every true Christian evangelist throughout church history. That apostolic passion was most clearly articulated by the apostle Paul as he wrote to the believers in the ancient city of Corinth. Speaking for all gospel workers, he said, "Now then, we are ambassadors for Christ, as though God were pleading through us: we implore you on Christ's behalf, *be reconciled to God*. For He made Him who knew no sin to be sin for us, that we might become the righteousness of God in Him" (2 Cor. 5:20–21 NKJV, emphasis added).

Biblically, damage to our relationships on the horizontal, or human, plane follows damage to our relationship on the vertical plane; that is, our relationship with God. We can see this in the

Genesis account of the entrance of sin into the original creation. In the beginning, Adam and Eve had a perfect relationship with God and with each other. But then the tempter entered the garden. He didn't start a marital fight; he led them to disobey a clear command of the Creator, one with a death penalty attached.

Once they had eaten the forbidden fruit, their relationship with God was badly damaged. However, their relationship with each other was obviously damaged, too. They made clothes to hide themselves from each other. There was a new hostile stance toward the other. Adam was quick to blame Eve for getting them in trouble with the Maker. Sadly, this was only the beginning of trouble on planet earth. Before long one of their sons would murder his brother.

I think it significant that the Ten Commandments start with commands concerning our relationship with God. Then they move to our relationships with one another. I suggest that we cannot mess up our relationships with one another without first messing up our relationship with the Maker. Thus, keeping our relationship with God in right condition helps us keep other relationships right. Get your relationship with God wrong, and you are bound to get your relationship with others wrong. I do not mean that everything about every relationship will be wrong, just that *some* things will certainly be wrong.

Reconciliation with God begins with the recognition that we are not reconciled, that the relationship is damaged—damaged by sin, our sin. We must first see that we have broken His commandments—maybe not all of them, but at least just one of them.

Breaking His commandments, however, breaks our relationship with Him. Our relationship is thus damaged and needs repair.

If we have been ignoring God, our relationship is damaged. He made us to notice Him and appreciate Him, not just obey His rules. The Bible says, "The heavens declare the glory of God; the skies proclaim the work of his hands. Day after day they pour forth speech; night after night they display knowledge. There is no speech or language where their voice is not heard. Their voice goes out into all

Be Reconciled To God

the earth, their words to the end of the world" (Ps. 19:1–4). Some of those words are, "There is a divine creator. He is awesome. He is an incredible designer, engineer, and maker. He is an artist of the highest order."

God made us with a capacity to know Him. He is powerful and He speaks. We are wise to seek Him. That is what brought Abraham such great honor. Believing that God "exists and that He rewards those who earnestly seek Him (Heb. 11:6), Abraham sought the Maker, and the Maker responded to his search. From this man Abraham, whom the Bible calls the "father of all who believe" (Rom. 4:11), comes a multitude of seekers who have found the one true God.

To begin restoring your relationship with God requires that you become a serious seeker of God. This is in contrast to being a hider from, an ignorer of, a denier of, or even a flirter with God. God delivered a specific word through the Hebrew prophet Jeremiah about the kind of seeking He desires; it is not to be lackadaisical, but purposeful. God said, "You will seek Me and find Me when you search for Me with all your heart" (Jer. 29:13 NKJV). Halfhearted seeking will never produce the desired results.

If you would be reconciled to God, you must not only engage in an honest and earnest search for God, but you must also deal with the offenses you have created by ignoring Him, hiding from Him, or denying Him. While in that disposition, you obviously were not obeying Him. Your acts of disobedience and insubordination are offensive to God. So are mine. So, what do we do about it? Fortunately, we don't do much. That is the good news we have in Christ.

You likely know that Jesus died on a cross; *everyone* does. But do you know *why* He died on a cross? Not everyone does know that. It was to effect reconciliation between God and us. Scripture tells us it was part of the divine plan from the very beginning; that is, the rebellion of mankind was not a shock to the Maker. The plan to restore rebellious mankind was worked out ahead of the actual need to do so (see Eph. 1:3,4). That plan included the eternal Son of God being born of a woman, thus being both man and God. That should be familiar to almost anyone. It is the story of Jesus—Immanuel, God with us (Matt. 1:23).

As a man, Jesus did what none of us could do. He obeyed the Father in every way. He was tested just like you and I are tested, yet where we have succumbed, He overcame (Heb. 4:15). Eventually, Jesus bore the punishment for all sinners. That is what happened on the cross. The Innocent One took the punishment due the guilty ones. The apostle Paul expressed this truth this way: "For he made him who knew no sin to be sin for us, that we might become the righteousness of God" (2 Cor. 5:21). That is what transpired on the cross of Calvary. We do not have to understand how the death of the absolutely innocent Jesus settles things in the heart of God related to our disobedience. We only need to trust this is true.

To be reconciled to God, therefore, means placing faith in Jesus and His reconciling transaction on our behalf. On the cross Jesus paid our sin debt; He settled our account with heaven. Furthermore, He proved the love of God for sinful mankind. God wants restored relationship with us. He has done the really hard part. What He expects of us is the honest confession that we are responsible for the damage to our relationship with Him. We have broken His laws and broken His heart.

Prophets often portrayed our relationship with God as that of a cheating wife to a faithful husband. Wanting to help us understand how our sin affects His heart, many times God called our sin "adultery." If we are honest with ourselves and with God, we can confess (agree with Him) that we have been unfaithful to Him, that He deserved much better from us than we have given, and that we have amassed a debt we cannot pay. We can turn from (repent of) ignoring, hiding from, or denying the Maker and His moral laws. This change of heart means we are ready to engage in a new relationship of faithfulness. We make our new relationship public; He is our Lord, and we are unashamed of this.

Baptism has been a significant role in Christian conversion since the gospel was first preached by Peter on the day of Pentecost. In our conversion, *we aren't just turning over a new leaf; we're starting a new life*. Thus, the terminology related to baptism, and even the original *mode* of baptism (immersion in water), portrays a death, burial, and resurrection. The new believer is lowered into water (as in a grave), and then he or she is raised out of the water (as in a resurrection). Consider these words of the apostle Paul about believer baptism: "Therefore we were buried with Him through baptism into death, that just as Christ was raised from the dead by the glory of the Father, even so we also should walk in newness of life. For if we have been united together in the likeness of His death, certainly we also shall be in the likeness of His resurrection" (Rom. 6:4–5 NKJV).

To be reconciled to God, then, is to recognize that we are at odds with God until we deal honestly with our sin and rebellion against Him. It is to look at the cross and see how seriously God regards our sin. It is to see the mercy of God manifested on that cross. It is to realize that God has offered forgiveness. It is to recognize the invitation to restored relationship with the Creator. It is to humbly come in repentance to receive what is offered in Jesus Christ. It is to commit oneself to following Jesus as Lord and thereby walk in newness of life.

Evangelicals have rightly stressed that Christianity is not so much about a religion as it is about a relationship. To be reconciled to God is to have our relationship with God restored. When this happens, we live our daily lives in the context of our relationship to Him. Just as a married person goes through daily experiences with an abiding awareness of experiencing these things as a married person (not as a single person) even when the spouse is not physically present, the Christian should live his or her life with an abiding awareness that whatever is experienced is as a redeemed child of God.

That being said, it is important to note that having a reconciled relationship with God is not necessarily blissful. Walking by faith can be very difficult at times. When we walk in disobedience as believers, it pleases God no more than when we did it as unbelievers. It strains the relationship and calls for repentance on our part.

As believers, sometimes we are disappointed with God. We feel He has let us down by allowing some bad thing to happen to a "good person." Maybe He doesn't answer a prayer in the way we want, in the time we want. In our disappointment, we may distance ourselves in the relationship. We may decide not to talk to Him, not to walk with Him. He bids us, however, to lay down the sense of offense and trust Him. If we are in that reconciled relationship, we will find Him drawing us back to Himself. He may not keep us out of a valley, but He will be with us in it.

Among my favorite verses is this passage from Proverbs: "Trust in the Lord with all your heart and lean not on your own understanding; in all your ways acknowledge Him, and He will make your paths straight" (Prov. 3:5–6). This speaks of relationship with God. People of faith have always been encouraged to engage in this relationship. Christ simply took us to a new depth of relationship. There are two promises attached to our response to the gospel in repentance and baptism: we are promised forgiveness of our sins *and* the gift of the Holy Spirit (see Acts 2:38). Thus, we are equipped well for relationship with God. He moves into our hearts, and you can't get closer than that!

Have you been reconciled to God? Have you honestly walked through these crucial matters of the heart, or have you just joined a church? Do you have that relationship with your Maker that Jesus made possible? It is yours for the taking. If you are unsure about this, please pray about it and talk about it with a mature believer or pastor. Working out reconciliation on the horizontal plane will be much more effective once you have been reconciled on the vertical plane.

I mentioned that we can become disappointed with God and choose to distance ourselves from Him in our hurt. Is that you? Would you unclench your fists, open your hands, and release the resentments you have been holding on to? Would you make a point of sharing your disappointments with a mature follower of Jesus or perhaps a pastor? Invite them into your spiritual battle. It may be too big to win by yourself. The door to victory may be opened by your admission of this fact.

God loves you. More than you can comprehend, He loves you! Though He is your Master, He wants to be your friend. He may have called you to walk through a very long, deep, and pain-filled valley, but He has all of eternity to heal and restore and compensate you. He has promised that He will. Through one of His prophets, God said, "I will repay you for the years the locusts have eaten" (Joel 2:25). If we are not repaid the losses of this life in this life, repayment awaits us on the other side. Our pain in this life can be incredibly long-lasting, but it never needs to be everlasting. God has made the way for us to enter everlasting life. There is a time for us to have every tear wiped away. It will be *soon*, and it will be *forever*! Please, be reconciled to God.

THE AUTHOR'S INVITATION:

If you are interested in a Zoom meeting with the author where he teaches some of the principles in this writing, along with some additional material, contact him at staff.forhim@gmail.com. Use the subject line "Zoom teaching on Everyone's Job." We will invite you to submit specific questions you would like addressed, then let you know about the next availability and cost to enroll.

ABOUT THE AUTHOR

Dane Tyner grew up in north-central Indiana, the middle child of a fairly poor and very dysfunctional family. After graduating high school in the midsixties, he left home to serve his country in the US Navy for four years. While in the navy, he entered an ill-advised marriage, which lasted about eight years.

Dane earned his bachelor's degree from Oral Roberts University in the spring of 1979. There he studied church history, theology, and psychology. Following his graduation, he was ordained into Christian ministry by the elders of Bellaire Christian Church in Tulsa. He remarried in the fall of that year. While serving in the pastorate, Dane returned to college to pursue a master's degree in counseling psychology, earning that degree in 1990 from Northeastern State University in Oklahoma.

After fifteen years of local church pastoral ministry, Dane and his wife founded Home Improvement Ministry, Inc. in Tulsa to assist Bible-believing churches in their efforts to address the great spiritual, emotional, and relational needs of individuals and families in our day. Dane's passion is to help people live the Christian life well. To that end, he teaches, counsels, writes, and speaks as God provides opens doors.

Dane's approach to ministry is transdenominational. He makes genuine effort to reach across denominational lines to affirm and build unity in the body of Christ. Most of the doctrinal issues that separate believers of different camps tend to be irrelevant in the work of inner healing and relational healing, which is his passion. His philosophy of helping people could be called "truth therapy," whereby he helps people encounter and embrace truth that can set them free. His bedrock sources of truth are the written Word of God and the indwelling Spirit of truth.

Dane and Kathy have been married for forty-one years as of November 2020. Together they have four children, nine grandchildren, and a ton of friends.

ACKNOWLEDGMENTS

As I prepare to write this acknowledgment of indebtedness to others, I think of big events that are pulled off with the involvement of many people. The ones in charge want to acknowledge those efforts, and some people come to mind immediately; but then there is the fear that someone will be left out—and hurt that they were left out. Unfortunately, in those settings, often someone is left out, unacknowledged, and hurt. I definitely don't want to damage any relationship here in my attempts to acknowledge those who have been important in this work.

I will start with an acknowledgment of God. The Father, the Son, and the Holy Spirit deserve credit for my life, my gifts and ministry, my friends and associates, and my encouragers and supporters. The apostle Paul said it first, but I completely understand the position in life that generates this outlook: "by the grace of God I am what I am" (1 Cor. 15:10). Indeed, to God be the glory and the gratitude.

I am indebted to many teachers, too many to honor by name. Innumerable preachers, teachers, professors, and authors have helped shape my understanding of God's Word and God's people. I must, however, mention two special ministers. One is a pastor friend I encountered as a young Christian, Brother Don Ott. We met in the church he led in Fort Smith, Arkansas, in the early seventies. Ours is a friendship that is a gift of the Holy Spirit. For unexplainable reasons, a lasting connection was made when I assisted with a revival in his church as a lay musician. Eventually, we wound up attending ORU together. He participated in my ordination in May of 1979 and stood up with me when I married Kathryn in November of that year. The bonds of mutual love and respect have supported and encouraged me through tough times in ministry.

The other minister I must acknowledge is a dear man to me and my wife. He was our pastor before we married. He not only taught me much, but he also supported me through a couple of the toughest years of my life. Thank you, Pastor Jim Garrett. I have always felt your support and encouragement for me as a man, as an equipping minister in Christ's church, and as a writer. You, too, have been a great gift of the Holy Spirit.

I have already mentioned her, but my dear wife, Kathryn, deserves much more than mention. She is my life partner and my ministry partner, fulfilling her calling to be a minister's wife. She followed her first husband, Gary Meyers, to Brazil to serve as missionaries there. After his tragic hit-and-run death in 1973, she returned to the United States, worked for a national Christian youth ministry based in Tulsa at the time, and attended the same church in Tulsa as I, Bellaire Christian Church. At that little church, we first became great friends and eventually much more. Kathy has always believed in me, and we make a good team. Especially in my writing, she has been quite helpful. She is my first editor. She proofreads and critiques almost everything I write. Her input has been invaluable.

Two other ladies served me in editing this writing and deserve special acknowledgment. Both were ladies my wife and I met while at Bellaire Christian Church. At the time, Dorothy Morris worked in the publishing department of Oral Roberts University, typing and proofing syllabi for professors, and Carol Forester Edwards worked for the Oral Roberts Evangelistic Association as a writer. In my early years of pastoral ministry at Bellaire, Dorothy played the piano on our worship team, and Carol led our children's ministry. Though we all left that church behind decades ago, mutual affections have remained strong throughout the years, even while living in three separate states. Both Carol and Dorothy worked with me on the manuscript to fine-tune it. Thanks to both of you for your friendship and your investment in this writing. Your input was a great blessing indeed.

Finally, I acknowledge the valuable contribution of the editorial staff of Xulon Press. They provided excellent professional help to further fine-tune the manuscript.

CPSIA information can be obtained
at www.ICGtesting.com
Printed in the USA
LVHW101640210323
742158LV00005B/461